This book is to be returned on or before
the date stamped below.

ROMAN
MYTHS & LEGENDS

by John Snelling

Illustrated by Margaret Theakston

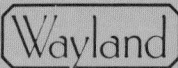

MYTHS AND LEGENDS

Celtic Myths and Legends
Greek Myths and Legends
Roman Myths and Legends
Viking Myths and Legends

Series Editor: Stephen Setford
Editor: William Wharfe

Consultant: Peter Dix (teacher of Classics at The King's School, Canterbury)
Designed by: DP Press, Sevenoaks, Kent

First published in 1988 by
Wayland (Publishers) Ltd
61 Western Road, Hove
East Sussex, BN3 1JD, England

British Library Cataloguing in Publication Data
Snelling, John, *1943–*
   Roman myths and legends. – (Myths and Legends).
   1. Mythology, Roman – Juvenile literature
   I. Title   II. Theakston, Margaret
   III. Series
   823'.914[J]   PZ7

ISBN 1–85210–272–1

Phototypeset by Kalligraphics Ltd, Redhill, Surrey
Printed by G. Canale & C.S.p.A., Turin
Bound by A.G.M., France

Contents

Introduction

Rome, the City of Seven Hills, is today the capital of just one country: Italy. But two thousand years ago it was the capital of a mighty empire that stretched from Britain to Egypt, from Spain to western Asia, from Germany to Africa.

The Romans used their power to enforce peace and civilization in the lands that they had conquered. Roman cities were supplied with fresh water, they had public baths, public theatres, and excellent roads to connect them with towns and other cities. Despite these benefits, Roman rule was in some ways very harsh – they made many people into slaves, and forced those who remained free to pay tax. Romans were not popular with everyone, but no one could afford to ignore them!

The Romans admired courage and loyalty. Many of their myths and legends praise these qualities. Other myths trace the beginnings of Rome in the mists of the distant past. Like all peoples the Romans liked to believe that their ancestors were very noble and important men and women. They even claimed that some were the children of gods and goddesses.

Destiny was very important to the Romans too. They believed that the gods controlled people's lives. It was therefore the sacred duty of each person to find out what the gods wanted of them – and to do it. You might try to fight against your Destiny, but you could never succeed.

The Romans worshipped the same gods and goddesses as the ancient Greeks, but they had different names for them. The one god that they alone worshipped was Janus. He was the god of beginnings. The first month of the year, January, is still named after him. Janus was believed to guard the doorways of Roman buildings so that no evil could get in. As he had two heads, he could face both inwards and outwards at the same time. It was also a Roman custom to close the gates of Janus' temple in the Forum when Rome was at peace. Sadly, those gates were almost never closed.

Above A Roman coin showing the head of the god Janus.

The Wanderings of Aeneas

This is a story of Aeneas – a man who led his people away from disaster to find a place to settle and build new homes. Aeneas was a nobleman of the city of Troy. His mother was Venus, goddess of love.

Long ago, there was a war between the Greeks and the Trojans. After ten years, the Greeks at last broke into the city of Troy and destroyed it, killing many Trojans.

Aeneas fought to defend his city as boldly as any Trojan. But finally he saw that the gods did not wish Troy to win. So, carrying his father Anchises on his shoulders and leading his son Ascanius by the hand, he left the burning city. Many other Trojans escaped too. Together they built ships and sailed away.

The Trojans eventually arrived at the island of Delos. There Aeneas went to the temple of Apollo, the god of prophecy. 'Great Apollo, we are weary,' he prayed. 'Please give us a new home. Where shall we look?'

At once the ground began to shake. 'Trojans – return to the land of your forefathers!' a great voice boomed.

At first they thought this meant the island of Crete. But after they had arrived there Aeneas had a dream. The Trojan gods appeared to him and said, 'Italy is our true home. Sail there.'

On his way to Italy, Aeneas stopped at Epirus. A noble Trojan named Helenus lived there. He was able to see into the future. 'After many adventures, you will see a huge white sow with thirty piglets,' Helenus told Aeneas. 'This will be a sign. Build your new home there. If you want to know more, go to Cumae. A wild woman called the Sybil lives there. She knows many secrets.'

Next Aeneas landed on the island of Sicily. Sadly, his father Anchises died there. More misfortune was in store. For when Aeneas tried to sail on to Italy, the goddess Juno, who hated all Trojans, threw a terrible storm in his path. This whirled his ships southwards to the shore of Africa. Here lay the city of Carthage.

Carthage was ruled by a beautiful queen named Dido. The goddesses Venus and Juno began to play tricks. They made Dido and Aeneas fall deeply in love with each other. Aeneas became so happy that he forgot all about looking for a new home. This made Jupiter, the greatest of all gods, very angry. He sent Mercury, his messenger, to Aeneas: 'You are forgetting your high Destiny. Think of the great nation you must found. You must set sail again.'

Aeneas knew that he must obey Jupiter. So he tried to slip away from Carthage without telling Dido. She found out, however. 'Traitor!,' she shouted angrily, and then began to cry and to beg him not to leave her.

Aeneas looked at Dido's beautiful
face. His heart was torn to see her
bitter tears. 'If I could choose, I
would stay,' he said sadly. 'But the
gods forbid it.' And he walked away
towards his ships.

Later Dido saw Aeneas' ships
sailing out of the harbour. Their
white sails were fat with the wind's
breath. Mad with sadness, Dido
killed herself.

Aeneas in the Underworld

When Aeneas at last landed in Italy, he went straight to see the Sybil of Cumae. He found her in a rocky cave beneath the Temple of Apollo. 'I wish to know more about my Destiny!' Aeneas told her.

At once the spirit of the god Apollo entered the Sybil. Possessed by the god, she began to foretell the future. 'I see war and all the horrors of war!' she screeched. 'I see the River Tiber foaming with blood! And all because a Trojan takes a foreign bride. But you must not draw back from the danger, Aeneas. You must strike on all the more daringly. . . '

The Sibyl then returned to normal. 'Now we will go to the Underworld to find out more,' she told Aeneas. 'I will guide you.'

What a horrible place the Underworld was! All murky and dark. The stench was dreadful too. Eerie cries echoed down its deep passageways. Horrible monsters, ghouls and ghosts appeared out of the gloom. There were lots of dead spirits there. But Aeneas was protected from these dangers – he carried a golden branch with special magic powers.

A hideous boatman named Charon ferried Aeneas and the Sibyl across a river in the Underworld known as the Styx. On the far side they met Cerberus, the three-headed hound of Hell. He was mad with hunger. Luckily the Sybil was able to put him to sleep with a drug.

Soon afterwards they arrived at the Fields of Mourning. Here the dead spirits wept sadly, for each had died of a broken heart. Queen Dido was among them. When she saw Aeneas, she turned away and wouldn't speak to him.

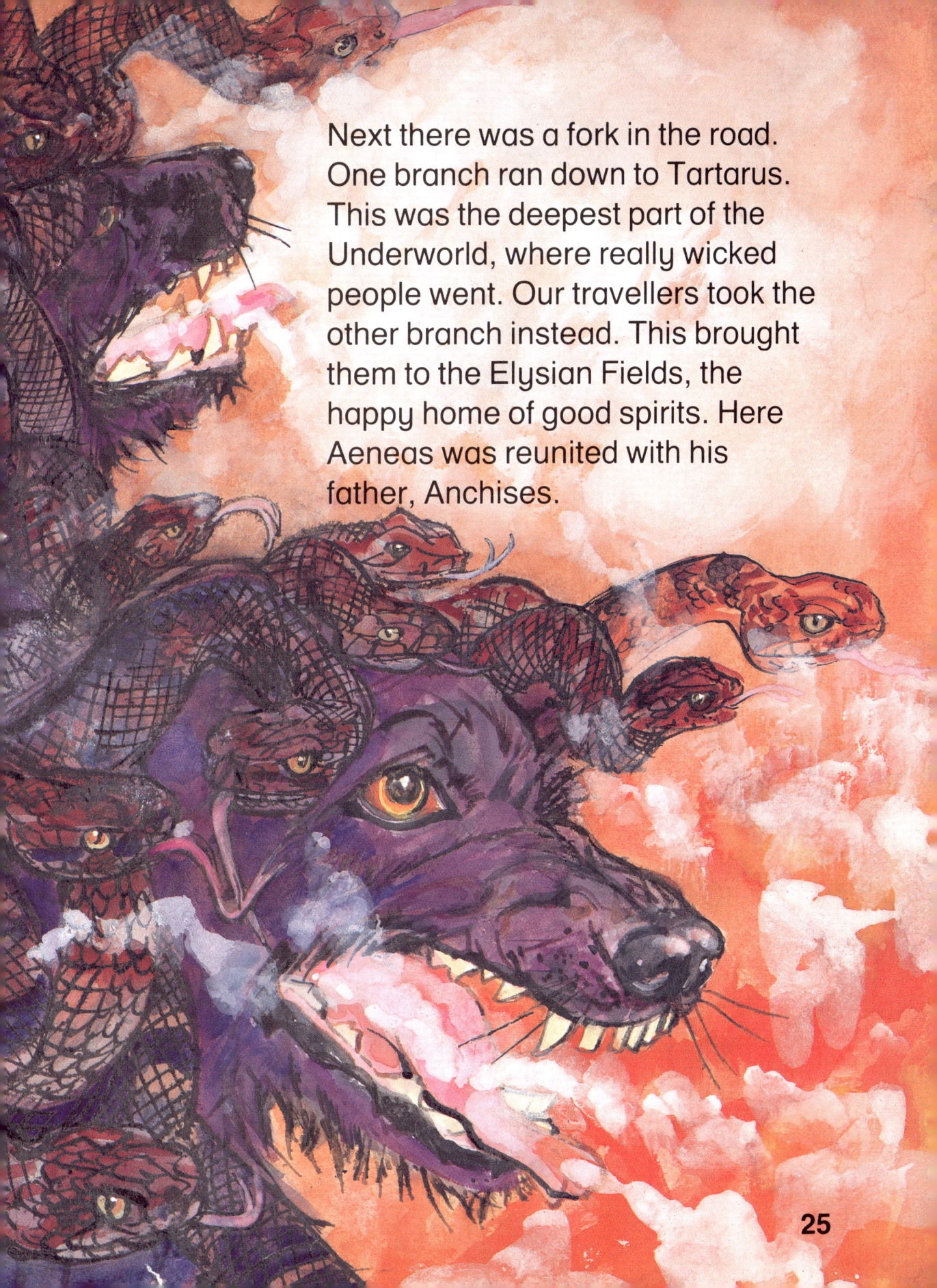

Next there was a fork in the road. One branch ran down to Tartarus. This was the deepest part of the Underworld, where really wicked people went. Our travellers took the other branch instead. This brought them to the Elysian Fields, the happy home of good spirits. Here Aeneas was reunited with his father, Anchises.

After hugging him, Anchises took Aeneas to the top of a hill in the Elysian Fields. Below, a huge crowd of souls were gathered. Some wore glittering armour. 'These are spirits than haven't been born yet,' Anchises told his son. 'They are your children and your children's children. Some of them will be the kings of the city of Alba. One of them, Romulus, will found the city of Rome. Rome will one day be the centre of one of the greatest empires the world will ever know. All this, Aeneas, is your Destiny . . .'

Afterwards, Aeneas left the Underworld and returned safely to his ships. He then sailed on up the coast of Italy. At last, at the mouth of the River Tiber, he saw a great white sow with thirty white piglets. Helenus had told him that this would mark the place for his new home. It lay in a region called Latium.

But shortly after arriving in Latium, just as the Sybil had foretold, war broke out. When Aeneas tried to marry Lavinia, the daughter of King Latinus, a prince named Turnus became jealous. He led an army against Aeneas. Turnus had many great warriors fighting for him, including the woman Camilla. She was stronger than many men and braver too. Despite her courage and strength, Camilla was one of the many killed in the terrible war between the Latins and the Trojans.

Finally, Aeneas and Turnus met each other in single combat.

'There is no turning back now, Turnus!' Aeneas cried. 'You must fight me, hand to hand!'

It was a long, hard fight, but in the end Aeneas won. Then he married Lavinia. This made the Trojans and the Latins into one people.

And afterwards all that Anchises had foretold did indeed come true — as you will see if you read on . . .

Romulus and Remus

Aeneas' sons and grandsons were kings of the city of Alba. There came a time when two brothers disagreed as to which of them was supposed to be king. Their names were Amulius and Numitor. In the end, Amulius made himself king and forced Numitor to leave the city.

One day King Amulius met Rhea Silvia, Numitor's daughter. 'She's very attractive,' he said to himself. 'One day she may get married. That could be a big problem for me. Her children might try to take revenge for what I've done to their grandfather.'

So Amulius ordered Rhea Silvia to become a Vestal Virgin. Vestal Virgins were not allowed to marry or have children. But later he found out that Rhea Silvia was expecting a baby.

'What!' Amulius cried with rage when he heard the news. 'Throw her in prison – at once!'

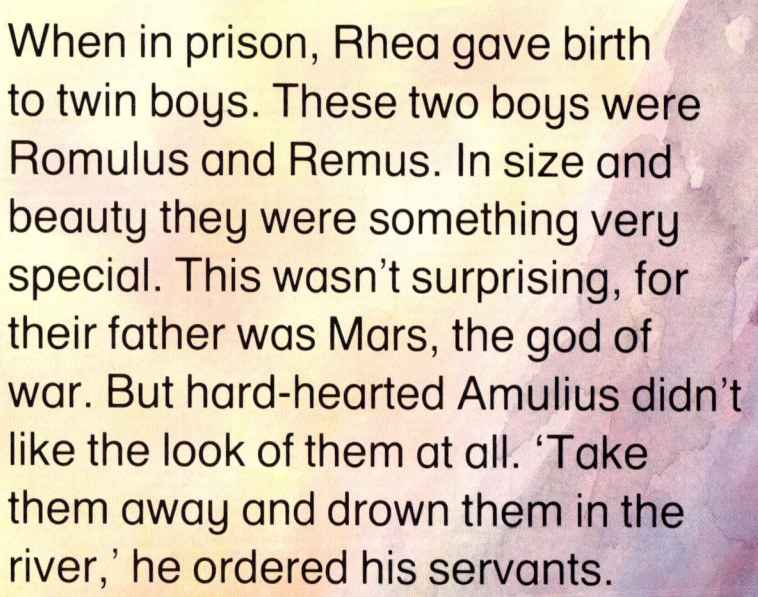

When in prison, Rhea gave birth to twin boys. These two boys were Romulus and Remus. In size and beauty they were something very special. This wasn't surprising, for their father was Mars, the god of war. But hard-hearted Amulius didn't like the look of them at all. 'Take them away and drown them in the river,' he ordered his servants.

When the servants reached the River Tiber, they were scared to go near because it had been raining and the river was flowing over its banks. So they just put the twins' cradle down on the bank and ran off. Later, the water rose and carried the cradle away. It was finally washed up near a wild fig tree called Ruminalis.

By this time, the baby twins hadn't had anything to eat for a long time, so they were crying loudly. A kind she-wolf heard them and let them drink the milk from her teats. Then a woodpecker flew down and helped to feed and guard them.

A little later a man named Faustulus happened to pass by. His job was to look after King Amulius' cattle. Faustulus was amazed to see the she-wolf licking the twins. When she had left the twins for a moment, Faustulus picked them up and carried them home to his wife, Larentia.

'Oh, aren't they lovely!' Larentia cried with delight. 'Let's keep them and look after them ourselves.'

So the twins were brought up by Faustulus and Larentia in a little hut.

When they were grown up, Romulus and Remus found out who they really were — and how King Amulius had tried to kill them. 'He'll pay for that!' they cried. So they killed him and made their grandfather, Numitor, king of Alba instead.

Next Romulus and Remus decided to found a city of their own. They wanted it to be near where the she-wolf had suckled them. Unfortunately they could not agree on the exact spot. So they asked the gods to give them a sign. They both saw vultures – lucky birds – flying in the sky.

'I saw them first!' cried Remus.

'But I saw more than you!' Romulus replied. And he began to build his city where he wanted. He called it Rome, after himself.

This annoyed Remus. He jumped over the half-built walls, crying, 'Useless walls you've got here, Romulus!'

A nasty scuffle broke out and Romulus killed Remus. 'The same thing will happen to anyone who leaps over my battlements!' Romulus cried.

Horatius at the Bridge

Tarquin the Proud was the last of the seven kings of Rome. And a nasty tyrant he was too. One day he turned up at the court of the Etruscan king of Clusium, Lars Porsena. Tarquin was in a very bad mood.

'Those wretched Romans have had the cheek to throw me out of the city!' he complained. 'You must help me win back my throne. After all, you and I are both of Etruscan blood.'

Tarquin told his story. But he didn't tell the whole truth: that the Romans had thrown him out because they had grown tired of his cruel wicked, ways.

'Yes, of course I will help,' Lars Porsena said. 'Call up my army. In thirty days we march on Rome!'

Lars Porsena's Etruscan army was very powerful indeed. It had soon captured the Janiculum Hill just outside Rome. From there it rushed down towards the *Pons Sublicius*, the one bridge that crossed the River Tiber. The Etruscans knew that if they captured it, Rome would be theirs.

Now the Roman soldiers panicked. They threw down their arms and ran away. Only one of them stood his ground – a brave captain named Horatius Cocles.

'We must chop down the bridge before the Etruscans reach it!' Horatius cried.

'Too late! Too late!' the others shouted.

'Then I shall defend it alone!' Horatius shouted back.

'You're crazy! Do you want to die?'

'We've all got to die some day,' Horatius replied. 'And there's no better way to go than fighting for our noble city and the temples of our gods!'

45

So, sword in hand, Horatius went out to meet the enemy. In a moment, two other brave men were at his side: Spurius Lartius and Titus Herminius. Swords clashed and spears whizzed. One mighty Etruscan warrior crashed into the dust. Then another . . . and another . . . and all the time, axes could be heard chopping away at the timbers down below.

At last the cry came: 'Save yourselves, the bridge is falling!'

Lartius and Herminius ran back. But Horatius stayed. He stood alone at the end of the bridge. 'Come on, you cowards!' he bellowed at the Etruscans. 'You've no more guts than a flock of sheep!'

The Etruscans were ashamed. They rushed at Horatius from all sides. The air was full of cries and clamour. And more Etruscans fell. . .

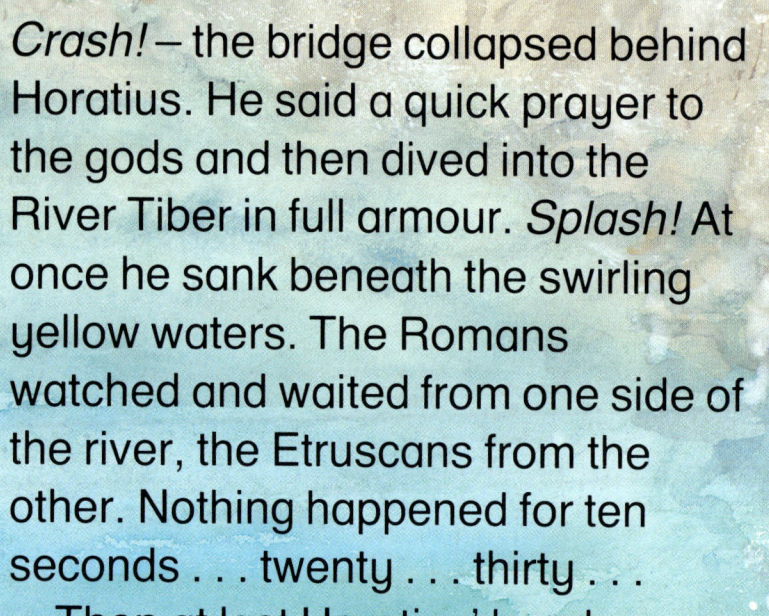

Crash! – the bridge collapsed behind Horatius. He said a quick prayer to the gods and then dived into the River Tiber in full armour. *Splash!* At once he sank beneath the swirling yellow waters. The Romans watched and waited from one side of the river, the Etruscans from the other. Nothing happened for ten seconds . . . twenty . . . thirty . . .

Then at last Horatius' head bobbed up. He began to swim to safety. *'Hooray!'* cried the Romans. And *'Hooray!'* cried the Etruscans – for they too could not help admiring this brave hero.

How the Geese Saved the Capitol

After Tarquin was driven out, Rome became a republic – this means it was ruled by men who were elected by the people of Rome.

Some time later, in 390BC, the armies of the Gauls marched southwards through Italy. The Gauls loved the sweet fruit and the bubbling wines of Italy. They conquered many Italian cities, including great Rome itself. The Capitoline Hill alone was not taken. This tall, steep rock was held by the bravest Roman fighters.

51

King Brennus, the leader of the Gauls, put guards around the Capitoline Hill. Then he went into the Forum. Here the oldest and wisest men of Rome sat in silence on ivory thrones. They looked like marble statues. The Gauls were amazed. 'They must be gods!' one whispered.

Then one Gaul put out his hand and pulled the white beard of one of the old men, Marcus Papirius. At once the noble Roman raised his staff and gave the cheeky Gaul a sharp blow on the head.

'*Agh!*' cried the Gaul. Enraged, he drew his sword and killed Marcus Papirius. Then the Gauls slaughtered all the Roman elders there in the Forum.

Now a desperate message was sent to Marcus Furius Camillus. Camillus was a famous general who had won great victory in battle. He had once been made Dictator, which meant that he was in charge of Rome. But he was both harsh and stubborn. This had made him unpopular, so he had been forced to go away from Rome. Yet, now that they were in trouble, the Romans wanted him back. The message to Camillus said, 'Rome has need of you. Become Dictator again.'

'I cannot go until all the Romans on top of the Capitoline Hill have elected me,' Camillus replied.

So a brave man named Pontius Cominius went to Rome. In the dead of night, he climbed the Capitoline Hill. The Romans up there agreed that Camillus should be asked to be Dictator again. Cominius took this message back to Camillus.

One of the Gauls had sharp eyes. He discovered the marks that Cominius had made when he had climbed the cliff.

'The enemy have shown us that there is a way of climbing this rock,' King Brennus said when he heard about this. 'Tonight – at midnight . . .'

A small party of Gauls made the climb in the dark. It was tough going. The cliff was very steep.

When the first Gaul reached the top, he looked around. All was quiet. 'They're all in bed asleep,' he murmured to himself.

But just at that moment a loud quacking started up, '*Qua-Qua-Qua . . . Qua-Qua-Qua . . .*' It was the geese that were kept in the temple of Juno. They ran about, flapping their wings and making the most terrible racket!

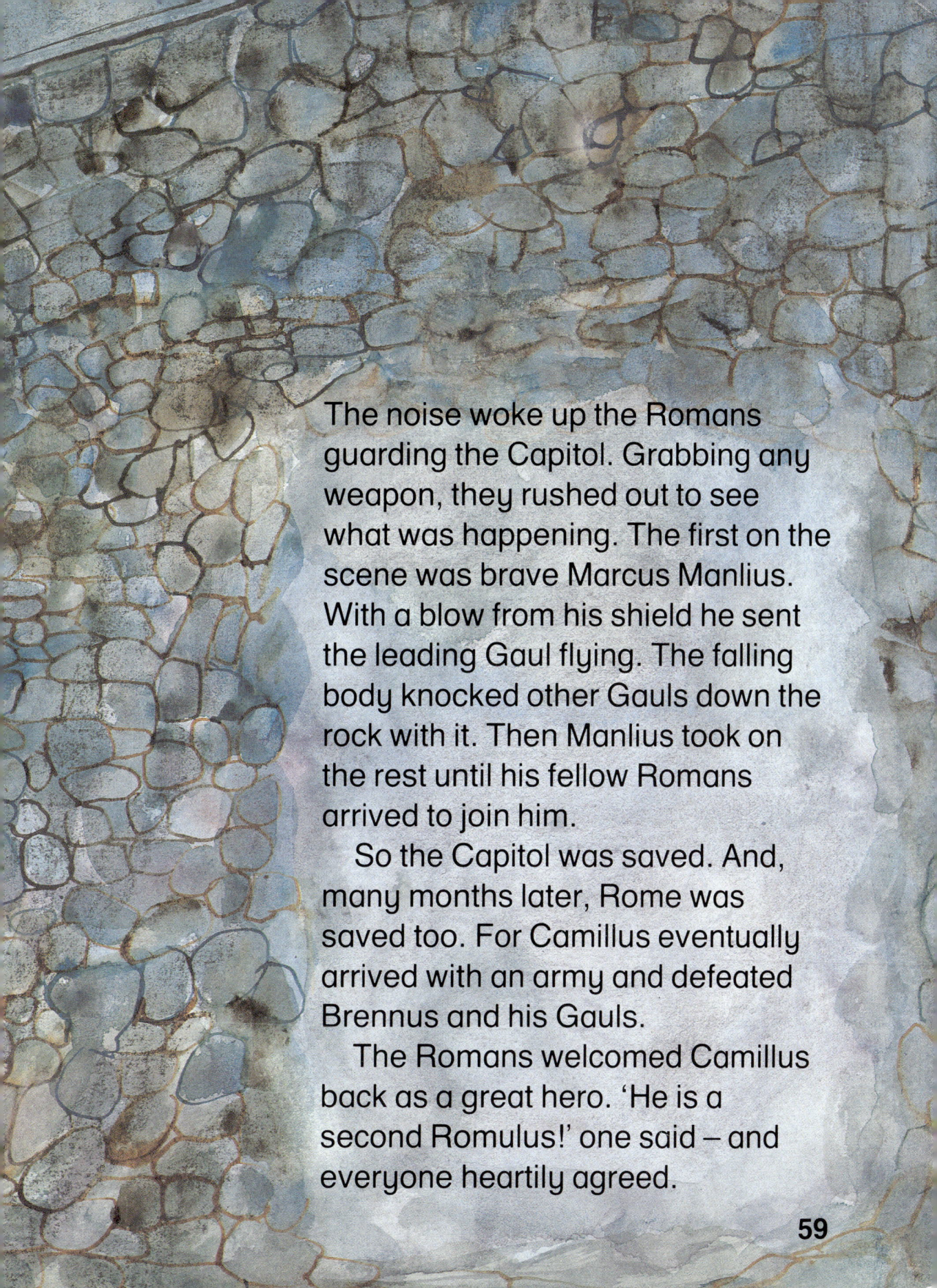

The noise woke up the Romans guarding the Capitol. Grabbing any weapon, they rushed out to see what was happening. The first on the scene was brave Marcus Manlius. With a blow from his shield he sent the leading Gaul flying. The falling body knocked other Gauls down the rock with it. Then Manlius took on the rest until his fellow Romans arrived to join him.

So the Capitol was saved. And, many months later, Rome was saved too. For Camillus eventually arrived with an army and defeated Brennus and his Gauls.

The Romans welcomed Camillus back as a great hero. 'He is a second Romulus!' one said – and everyone heartily agreed.

List of Characters and Places

Aeneas   Father of the Roman people. A Trojan prince who eventually settled in Latium in Italy.

Alba Longa   A Latin city founded before Rome by Aeneas' son Ascanius.

Amulius   Brother of Numitor, whom he ousted to become king of Alba. Uncle of Romulus and Remus.

Anchises   Father of Aeneas.

Apollo   The god of prophecy.

Brennus   The king of the Gauls who took Rome in around 390BC.

Camilla   A woman warrior who fought for Turnus against the Trojans.

Camillus, Marcus Furius   A great general and Dictator of the Roman Republic.

Capitoline Hill   One of the Seven Hills of Rome, where the Temple of Jupiter stood.

Carthage   A Phoenician city in North Africa.

Cerberus   The terrible three-headed hound of Hell.

Crete   An island in the Mediterranean Sea.

Dido   Queen of Carthage.

Epirus   An ancient country in northwestern Greece.

Etruscans   The people of Etruria, a region of ancient Italy just north of Rome.

Gauls   A Celtic people who, in around 390BC, invaded Italy.

Cocles, Horatius   The brave Roman captain who defended the bridge (*Pons Sublicius*) against the Etruscan army.

Janus   The two-headed Roman god of beginnings.

Juno   The queen of the gods. Wife of Jupiter.

Jupiter   The king of the gods.

Mars   The god of war.

Mercury   The messenger of the gods.

Numitor   The father of Rhea Silvia. He became king of Alba after his brother Amulius was killed by his grandsons, Romulus and Remus.

Porsena, Lars   The Etruscan king of Clusium.

Remus   Son of Rhea Silvia by Mars. Twin brother of Romulus.

Romulus   Son of Rhea Silvia by Mars. Twin brother (and murderer) of Remus.

Silvia, Rhea   Daughter of Numitor. Mother of Romulus and Remus.

Styx, River   One of the rivers of the Underworld.

Tarquin the Proud   (L. Tarquinius Superbus) A tyrant. Last king of Rome. Deposed c. 510BC.

Tartarus   The lowest pit of the Underworld, where the Romans believed evil people ended up.

Turnus   An Italian prince who fought with Aeneas – and died by his hand.

Venus   The goddess of love.

Glossary

Destiny According to the Romans, this was the shape of a person's life as laid down by the gods.

Dictator A ruler who has complete power. His word is law.

Forum The place of assembly in Rome.

Hades The ancient name for the Underworld.

Mourning The sadness people feel when someone they have loved dies.

Prophecy A prediction of future events.

Republic A country ruled by its people and those whom they elect.

Sibyl A prophetess or woman who can foretell the future.

Tyrant A cruel and wicked ruler.

Vestal Virgins The priestesses who looked after the sacred fire in the Temple of Vesta in Rome. They did not marry or have children.

Textual Notes

The stories in this book are concerned with events during the earliest phases of Roman history and prehistory. The first Roman historian (Quintus Fabius Pictor) was writing about 550 years after Romulus was supposed to have founded Rome. Hence there was a lack of evidence which had to be made up for by using imagination and other (usually Greek) legends.

The legend of Aeneas, with which our first two stories are concerned, is the central Roman myth. Essentially fictional, it owes much to Greek mythology. It is possible to discern elements of Homer's *Odyssey* and *Iliad* in Aeneas' wanderings and in the warfare in Italy in the second part of the story. The principal source for the story is the epic poem, *Aeneid*, by the Latin poet Virgil (70–19 BC). The *Aeneid* ties the Romans into the Greek world by tracing their origins back to Aeneas and Troy. That Aeneas could claim the goddess Venus as his mother would confer additional prestige upon Rome and especially upon Virgil's contemporary the Emperor Augustus, who according to the *Aeneid* was related to Aeneas.

There are several accounts of the foundation of Rome. Our version is based on that by Plutarch in his *Lives*. However, numerous variations of the story exist. The marvellous tale of Romulus and Remus is similar to that of Neleus and Pelias, sons of Poseidon, who were exposed on a river bank and suckled by a bitch and a mare.

The story of Horatius occurs in various versions: besides Polybius (in which Horatius meets a watery end), there also exist fragments of the treatments by Fabius Pictor and Ennius. Our retelling is based on Livy and is strongly influenced by the epic poem by Lord Macaulay, published in his *Lays of Ancient Rome* (1842). It should be noted that the legend is based around the historical banishment of Tarquinius Superbus around 510BC, and that despite Horatius' bravery, Lars Porsena probably did in fact conquer Rome.

Our version of the legend featuring the geese saving the Capitol is based mainly on Plutarch's *Life of Camillus* and Livy's account in book five of his *History of Rome*. It is historically probable that the Capitol as well as the rest of Rome fell to Brennus' Gauls and that they left the city undefeated, of their own accord. To offset the humiliation of the event, historians rewrote history and worked in or exaggerated heroic deeds performed by the Romans.

Further Reading

For Teachers

Grant, Michael, *Roman Myths* (Penguin, 1973)

Livy, *History of Rome* (trans) B.O.Foster, F.G. Moore, E.T. Sage and A.C. Schlesinger. Loeb Classical Library (Heinemann, 1929)

Macaulay, Thomas B., *Lays of Ancient Rome* (Longman, 1842)

Ogilivie, R.M., *A Commentary on Livy, Books 1–5* (Oxford University Press, 1965)

Ovid, *Metamorphoses* (trans) Mary M. Innes (Pengiun, 1955)

Plutarch, *Lives* (trans) Bernadotte Perrin. Loeb Classical Library (Heinemann, 1914)

Virgil, *The Aeneid* (trans) W.F. Jackson Knight (Penguin, 1978)

Williams, R.D., *Aeneas and the Roman Hero*, Inside the Ancient World series, (Macmillan, 1973)

For Pupils

Corbishley, Mike, *The Roman World* (Kingfisher Books, 1986)

Croft, Peter, *The All-colour Book of Roman Mythology* (Octopus Books, 1974)

Sorrell, Alan, and Birley, Anthony, *Imperial Rome* (Lutterworth, 1970)

Sutcliff, Rosemary, *The Eagle of the Ninth* (Penguin, 1954)